S0-AYV-337

To Our Mothers,

We apologize.

Acknowledgments

We'd like to recognize the contributions and help of Steve Harwood, Jonah Van Zandt, Chris DeSena, Chris Schultz, Todd DeHart, Steve A, Paul Katz, Lizbet Traks, Megan Incorvaia, Rick Foss, and anyone else who sent us questions that we unconsciously stole. Thanks to all the WYR fans for your support.

Thank you to Davey-Boy Smith for your business casual acumen. Thanks to Jay Mandel for believing in all of our delusions. Thanks to Tom Schirtz—we are all mere pawns of your Design.

Gomberg: While I'll never be able to compete with the Great Kabuki's in-the-ring prowess, you still found a way to fall in love with me. Sophia, you are my wife and my life.

Heimberg: Thank you, Marisa, for giving me reason to permanently retire that forlorn author photo. I promise that some day I will have a real book to dedicate to you. I love you.

Contents

A Note from the Authors

We tried. We made an honest effort to maintain our artistic integrity during our 20's. We tried to expand our literary oeuvre beyond "read'em and wipe" humor books, to experience the world, to expound upon our journeys with acute observations and penetrating insights. Yet ten years later, we find ourselves having come full circle, our noble efforts proven fruitless. Gomberg's attempt at a 17 book volume of criticism of the poetry of John Donne was met with tepid reactions from commercial publishers. Meanwhile, Heimberg floundered in his attempt to write a series of mystery novels based on the characters of Bartles and Jaymes. And so then, to address fiscal strains (Gomberg has 6 children with 7 different mothers; Heimberg continues to struggle with his financially draining snuff habit), we again find ourselves slumming in the world of a genre that can only be deemed the oxymoronic "Juvenile Adult," ambitious dreams of healing the world through writing now diminished to a fading hope to write the Great American Fart Joke.

Enjoy!

How to use this book

Sit around with a bunch of friends and read a question to each other, discussing it until the momentum of the conversation fades into awkward silence and nervous glances. Everybody must choose. As the Deity proclaims, **YOU MUST CHOOSE!** That's the whole premise of this thing. It forces you to really think about the options. Once everyone has chosen, move on to the next question. It's that simple. We have provided a few things to consider when deliberating each question, but don't restrict yourself to these topics, as much of the fun comes from imagining the different ways your choice will affect your life. If you receive a question directed at females, and you are a male (or vice-versa), you can do one of several things: a) move on to another question, b) answer the question anyway, or c) panic.

chapter ONE

CURSES

These are the circumstances: A deity descends from on high and informs you that, for reasons beyond your understanding, your sex life is about to change. From this unfortunate moment on, regarding matters of the flesh and heart, you are to be plagued with a terrible curse—a bizarre behavioral disorder, an outrageous physical deformity, or an irksome inconvenience. The Deity is not without compassion however. He allows you to choose between two possible fates.

Would you rather...

orgasm once every ten years

OR

once every ten seconds?

Things to consider: business meetings, funerals, dry cleaning bills

Would you rather...

have commercial interruptions during masturbation fantasies

OR

have to masturbate with the mandatory use of a *Sesame Street*'s Elmo hand puppet?

YOU MUST CHOOSE!

Would you rather...

have your genitalia located on the palm of your left hand OR the front of your neck?

on the middle of your back OR on your elbow?

on your hip OR your ankle?

Things to consider: oral sex, masturbation, custom tailoring

YOU MUST CHOOSE!

3

Would you rather...

have breast implants made of Nerf *OR* Play-Doh?

quarters *OR* brie cheese?

thumb tacks *OR* tadpoles?

helium *OR* Pillsbury Dough-boys?

YOU MUST CHOOSE!

Would you rather...

have to have sex in the same position every night

OR

have to have sex in a different position every night (you can never repeat)?

Things to consider: cowgirl, reverse cowgirl, pile driver, reverse pile driver, doggie-style, penguin-style, missionary, rabbinical missionary, the startled spelunker, the Van Zandt spin, 69, 96, 55, 127, 00 (aka the Robert Parish)?

YOU MUST CHOOSE!

Would you rather...

have a penis that sheds skin like a snake every week

OR

a penis that makes the sound of a rainstick when it moves?

Would you rather...

have to use condoms two times too big *OR* two times too small?

aluminum foil condoms *OR* the same condom over and over?

condoms covered in sandpaper *OR* condoms covered with pictures of your mother?

YOU MUST CHOOSE!

Would you rather...

have a neurological abnormality that causes you to appeal victoriously to an imaginary crowd à la Hulk Hogan after sex

OR

have a condition where as soon as you see someone take their clothes off, you point to the "appropriate" body parts and say quite suavely, "milk, milk, lemonade, 'round the corner fudge is made"?

YOU MUST CHOOSE!

Would you rather...

every hour on the hour, change which gender you are attracted to

OR

turn your sexual partner into Tony Danza when you climax, and then turn them back to themselves the next time you have sex with them?

Things to consider: maintaining a marriage, determining who the boss is

YOU MUST CHOOSE!

Would you rather...

utter all exclamations during sex in Yiddish *OR* Chinese?

in sign language *OR* in the form of a question as if on *Jeopardy*?

in Pig Latin *OR* with IM acronyms?
Things to consider: rabgay hattay itttaytay; lol, brb, ftp, diithbh, ccr, elo, bto

YOU MUST CHOOSE!

Would you rather...

ejaculate a deadly dart

OR

die if you are not having sex at 3:37 pm every day?

Things to consider: moving to Vegas, pulling out, work as a spy, self defense

YOU MUST CHOOSE!

Would you rather...

see in ColecoVision graphics quality when having sex

OR

have to use clinical terms during dirty talk?
(for example, "Penetrate that vagina!"; "Lick that mons pubis!";
"Ram that glans against the epidermis of the uvula!")

YOU MUST CHOOSE!

Would you rather...

everything you say be considered an insult

OR

a come-on?

Would you rather...

have dreadlocked pubes

OR

have nipple-itis (constant visibly erect nipples that show through anything you wear)?
Things to considers: tuxedoes, the beach, short shorts

YOU MUST CHOOSE!

The Deity, though known to have assumed corporeal form to rape mortals and livestock, is a believer in safe sex for you. Sort of...

Would you rather your only means of birth control be...

gum *OR* an English Muffin?

a rubber band and a box of tic-tacs *OR* a roll of "Jazz Icon" postage stamps?

a waffle cone *OR* anal sex?

a stapler *OR* an 8"x10" photograph of Wilfred Brimley?

YOU MUST CHOOSE!

Mood Music

The Deity is going to help you set the mood with something from his private music collection.

Would you rather...

always have to have sex to Arab prayer music OR ragtime music?

"Oklahoma" OR "Swing Low, Sweet Chariot?"

The Lone Ranger Theme OR "Wipeout?"

"99 Red Balloons" OR "99 Luftballons?"

vocabulary builder CD's OR a loop of Louis Gosset Jr. coughing?

YOU MUST CHOOSE!

Would your rather...

have orgasms that feel like a brain-freeze

OR

be able to maintain an erection (men)/reach orgasm (women) only by accurately reciting the digits of Pi (you have to start over if you mess up)?

Things to consider:
3.14159265358979323846264338327950288419716939937510582097494459230781640628620899862803482534211706798214808651328230664709384460955058223172535940812848111745028410270193852110555964462294895493038196442881097566593344612847564823378678316527120190914564856692346034861045432664821339360726024914127372458700660631558817488152092096282925409171536436789259...

YOU MUST CHOOSE!

Pick Your Penis!

Would you rather have...

(women, read the following questions as "have a partner with")

a 4 inch long penis with a 2 inch diameter **OR** an 8 inch penis with a half inch diameter?

an 8 inch penis that was always soft **OR** a 3 inch penis that was always hard?

a retractable penis **OR** a detachable penis?

a penis able to drink like an elephant uses his trunk **OR** a penis that glows in the dark when you twist the head?

Things to consider: pitching a tent at night

YOU MUST CHOOSE!

Would you rather have...

(women, read the following questions as "have a partner with")

a two-pronged penis **OR** a right angle penis?

an invisible penis **OR** a penis that turns green and tears out of your clothing like the Incredible Hulk every time you get aroused?

a Rubik's Snake penis **OR** a penis that can act as a light saber upon your command?

Things to consider: doctors' waiting rooms, abuse of power

YOU MUST CHOOSE!

Would you rather...

ejaculate guacamole *OR* Tabasco sauce?

Scope *OR* crazy string?

air-rifle bb's *OR* high voltage electric shocks?

confetti *OR* baseball umpire strike and ball calls?

through your nostrils *OR* through your eyes?

YOU MUST CHOOSE!

Would you rather your only porn be...

6 second clips of hot people *OR* 2 minute clips of moderately attractive people?

verbose, subtle erotic fiction *OR* pornographic Magic Eye 3D pictures (the ones where you have to stare just right until the image comes into focus)?

Spanish channel variety shows *OR* vague, slightly inaccurate recollections of a 1980's Markie Post?

animal nature documentaries *OR* suggestive cloud formations?

geometric shapes *OR* family reunion pictures?
Things to consider: the arousing rhombus

YOU MUST CHOOSE!

chapter **TWO**

YOUR WILDEST FANTASIES

Our rather bipolar Deity, it appears, is in a good mood. Something about a sacrifice. Consequently, he's going to offer you the chance to fulfill one of your wildest—or at least, his wildest—fantasies. Even more uncharacteristically magnanimous, he's going to give you a choice between two.

Would you rather have sex with...

Russell Crowe *OR* Pierce Brosnan?

Johnny Depp *OR* George Clooney?

Clay Aiken *OR* Ruben Studdard?

C3PO *OR* R2D2?

YOU MUST CHOOSE!

Would you rather have sex with...

Gwen Stefani *OR* Jennifer Aniston?

Cameron Diaz *OR* Alyssa Milano?

the new Daisy Duke (Jessica Simpson) *OR* classic Daisy Duke (Catherine Bach)?

Rebecca Romijn *OR* Rebecca Romijn-Stamos?

YOU MUST CHOOSE!

Would you rather have phone sex with...

Donald Trump OR Alf?

Hardball's Chris Matthews OR the narrator from all those movie trailers?

Shakespeare OR Dr. Seuss?

Yoda OR Bob Ross (the calm "Happy Trees" painter from PBS)?

a severe stutterer OR someone who has a sexy voice but uses fifth grade terms like "boobie," "tushy," "pee-pee," and "bagina" for sex words?

Marcel Marceau OR the dog from the old Snausages commercials?

YOU MUST CHOOSE!

Would you rather have phone sex with...

Dr. Laura Schlessinger *OR* Martha Stewart?

Condoleezza Rice *OR* Hillary Clinton?

Barbara Streisand *OR* the ghost of Harriet Tubman?

someone who constantly corrects your grammar *OR* someone prone to quoting Joseph Goebbels throughout?

Gary Gnu *OR* Pegasus?

YOU MUST CHOOSE!

Would you rather...

have a mountain range named after you

OR

have a sexual position officially named after you?

YOU MUST CHOOSE!

Would you rather...

have sex with a guy who has the body of John Goodman and the face of Brad Pitt

OR

or the body of Brad Pitt and the face of Mayor McCheese?

Would you rather...

have sex with a woman that has the body of Janet Reno and the face of Angelina Jolie

OR

the body of Angelina Jolie and the face of former Milwaukee Buck Jack Sikma?
Things to consider: doggie-style

YOU MUST CHOOSE!

Would you rather...

have sex with a 10 *OR* two 5's? (5's are at the same time)

a 10 *OR* ten 1's?

a 10 with syphilis *OR* a 4 with nice high thread count sheets?

a 10 and a -3 *OR* a 5?

Siamese twin 10's *OR* just one 10?

$10^2 - \left(2 + \sqrt{125/9}\right)$ *OR* $2^{4(32 - .65)}$?

Things to consider: order of operations

YOU MUST CHOOSE!

Would you rather have sex with...

Gwyneth Paltrow *OR* Carmen Electra with a unibrow?

a toothless Kelly Clarkson *OR* a hairless Lucy Liu?

Pamela Anderson *OR* a threesome with Natalie Portman and her clone?

an albino Eva Longoria *OR* Katie Holmes slathered in mayo?

Lindsey Lohan 30 years from now *OR* Lindsey Lohan 6 years ago?

Elizabeth Hurley without the accent *OR* Beyoncé Knowles without the accent (i.e. Beyonce Knowles)?

YOU MUST CHOOSE!

Would you rather live in a world where...

condoms were able to magically crawl out of the wrapper and put themselves on at exactly the right moment

OR

there was a male contraceptive pill that caused some bloating and moodiness?

YOU MUST CHOOSE!

Would you rather...

have sex with Tom Brady and get herpes

OR

have sex with Tim Russert and get a sensible but stylish tote bag?

Would you rather...

have sex with Jenna Jameson and get crabs

OR

have sex with Katie Couric and get a nice pair of business-casual wrinkle-free slacks with solid craftsmanship?

YOU MUST CHOOSE!

31

Ménage à Troiseses

Would you rather have a three-way with...

Flavor Flav and Teri Hatcher **OR** Ted Koppel and Kelly Ripa?

Jennifer Connelly and Lawrence Taylor **OR** Jennifer Garner and Nelson Mandela?

the Olsen twins **OR** the Wonder Twins?

the *Guinness Book of Records* World's Fattest Twins (the ones who are always shown on motorcycles) **OR** the *Guinness Book of Records* World's Tallest Man and World's Shortest Man?

Things to consider: Note to self: Idea for TV show: The fat twins on motorcycles become motorcycle cops; also: try to make sentence with as many colons as possible.

YOU MUST CHOOSE!

Would you rather...

get punched hard in the gut by the person on your left
OR
kissed passionately by the person on your right?

Would you rather have sex with...

a 5'2" version of Ashton Kutcher *OR* Jason Bateman if he put on 50 pounds?

a soft and tender Don Cheadle *OR* an excitingly rough Hamburglar?

Antonio Banderas without limbs *OR* Tobey Maguire with an extra one?

a chain-smoking Kofi Annan *OR* Ben Kingsley playing a kazoo?

YOU MUST CHOOSE!

Historical Friction

If you could go back in time, would you rather...

dance with Fred Astaire *OR* be serenaded by Frank Sinatra?

have Leonardo DaVinci paint your portrait *OR* have Shakespeare write you a sonnet?

have Mozart compose a symphony for you *OR* have Jeff Foxworthy compose a "You Might Be A Redneck If..." joke in your honor?

Would you rather...

get drunk-dialed by Gandhi
OR
by Martin Luther King?

YOU MUST CHOOSE!

Would you rather...

have sex with Paris Hilton

OR

punch her in the face?

Would you rather...

play Electronic Battleship with Tyra Banks

OR

help Michelle Kwan assemble a bookshelf?

YOU MUST CHOOSE!

Putting the "OR" in "ORgy"

Would you rather attend an orgy with...

The Mclaughlin Group *OR* the Fry Guys?

insincere horticulturalists *OR* conceited veterinarians?

obese clowns *OR* over-intrusive Gap sales staff?

The Keebler Elves *OR* the Rice Crispy Onomatopoeias?

YOU MUST CHOOSE!

Date, Marry, or Screw?

Here's an oldie but a goodie. We give you three names. You decide which one you'd marry, which you'd date, and which you'd screw.

Bill Clinton, George Bush, George Bush Sr.

Alec Baldwin, Stephen Baldwin, Daniel Baldwin

Michael Jackson circa *Thriller*, Michael Jackson circa *Bad*, Michael Jackson now

Britney Spears, Jessica Simpson, Mariah Carey

Condoleezza Rice, Connie Chung, the hot Hooters waitress with low self esteem

YOU MUST CHOOSE!

Date, Marry, Screw, Play Ping Pong Against, or Create a Revolutionary Movement With?

Okay, you mastered that one. Now to challenge you, we've added a few more options and names, resulting in more permutations. Here you must decide, which name you'd marry, which you'd date, which you'd screw, which you'd play ping-pong against, and which you would start a revolutionary movement with.

Ben Affleck, Matt Damon, Che Guevara, ping pong champion John Hu, Mel Gibson

Tommy Lee, Ben Franklin, Tim Duncan, The Rock, Alan Greenspan

Courtney Cox, Lisa Kudrow, Jennifer Aniston, Deborah Messing, your mother

Al Sharpton, Corey Feldman, Corey Haim, Venus Williams,
the girl at Starbucks who looks a little like Larry Bird

YOU MUST CHOOSE!

Pretty good, but can you handle this one?

Date, Marry, Screw, Discuss War of 1812 with, Accompany to Six Flags Amusement Park, or Collaborate to Write Hip Hop Album?

Jerome Bettis, Molly Ringwald, George Stephanopoulos, Eminem, Menudo, God

UN Ambassador John Bolton, 50 Cent, Tiger Woods, The Teletubbies, Patrick Swayze, Roberto Benigni

Maria Shriver, Bill Wennington, Darth Maul, Hitler, a can of tennis balls, Gomberg

YOU MUST CHOOSE!

39

Would you rather use as sex toys...

a tetherball, a map of Uruguay, and a menorah

OR

some measuring spoons, a thermos, and a Mark Eaton rookie card?

YOU MUST CHOOSE!

Pornification
By Andrew Ackerman

Pornographers are quick to capitalize on the success of mainstream movies. All it takes to turn an actual movie into a pornographic film is a slight tweak of the title. This process is called "**Pornification**."

For example,

Good Will Hunting, when pornified, becomes *Good Will Humping*.

Similarly, *The Terminator* becomes, of course, *The Sperminator*.

For every legit movie, there exists (at least theoretically) a porn version of that movie.

Test your understanding of **Pornification** on the next two pages with our **Pornification Quiz**.

YOU MUST CHOOSE!

Here are some pornified titles. Can you figure out the original Hollywood film that inspired them? Answers on page 167.

1. *American Booty*
2. *Titty Lickers*
3. *Grinding Nemo*

Now, the fun part. We give you the popular movie title. Can you pornify it? Answers on page 167.

4. *The Nutty Professor*
5. *S.W.A.T.*
6. *Toy Story*

YOU MUST CHOOSE!

More titles to pornify.

7. *Big Trouble in Little China*
8. *Analyze This*
9. *Glory*
10. *Space Jam*
11. *Malcolm X*
12. *Chitty Chitty Bang Bang*
13. *Shaft*
14. *Cold Mountain*
15. *Lou Dobbs Moneyline*

YOU MUST CHOOSE!

THE POWER OF LOVE

The Deity has decided to bestow upon you a sexual super-power. But, as Shakespeare said, "with great power, comes great responsibility." Choose wisely.

Would you rather...

be able to achieve orgasm at will

OR

be able to make anyone other than you achieve orgasm at your will?

Things to consider: public speakers, staff meetings, sporting events

YOU MUST CHOOSE!

Would you rather...

have genitalia that can function as a DustBuster

OR

nipples that can act as universal light dimmers?

Would you rather...

acquire all the knowledge of people you have sex with

OR

right before you climax, have the choice to store up orgasms to experience later, like the "downloading later" function on email?

Things to consider: rainy days, orgasm breaks at work, nerd-banging

YOU MUST CHOOSE!

Would you rather...

have puma-like reactions with the remote control when watching something dirty, and someone walks into the room, and you need to change it

OR

have expert precision with the cheek-kiss greeting?

Would you rather...

have a stable of remarkably sympathetic woodland creatures to confide in about romantic desires and dreams

OR

be capable of ending any relationship tension-free with no ensuing debate or discussion by pulling out a red card like in soccer?

Things to consider: yellow card warnings

YOU MUST CHOOSE!

Would you rather...

during sex, be able to read the mind of the person you are having sex with

OR

be able to hit your or your partner's g-spot by finding Waldo in a *Where's Waldo* book? (each page can be used once)

YOU MUST CHOOSE!

chapter **FOUR**

COOL AND UNUSUAL PUNISHMENT

The Deity is having a bad day, and he's decided to take it out on you. Why? Reasons beyond your understanding. Nonetheless, you are to undergo a terrible, horrific, Deity-awful experience—something painful, embarrassing, or downright disgusting. ☺

Would you rather...

have you parents walk in on you while you are having sex

OR

walk in on them?

Would you rather...

chew a used condom as gum for an hour

OR

have all your pubic hairs become ingrown?

YOU MUST CHOOSE!

After a night of drunkenness, would you rather wake up next to...

a close co-worker *OR* a friend of your mother's?

your best friend of the opposite sex *OR* your very attractive first cousin?

the ugliest person from your high school *OR* that freaky mascot dude in the Burger King commercials?

YOU MUST CHOOSE!

These are the circumstances. You are stuck on a desert island. You pray to the Deity, and he allows you one possession.

Would you rather be stuck on a desert island with...

the complete works of Jane Austen **OR** a year's worth of *Barely Legal*?

your significant other and an Ipod filled with Barry White's most sultry tunes **OR** your significant other and a complete set of *Magic: The Gathering* cards?

a fishing rod **OR** a funhouse mirror, a wig, and some KY jelly?

Socrates **OR** Jenna Jameson?

P-Diddy's wardrobe **OR** an unlimited supply of nude photos of Tony Feuerstein?

YOU MUST CHOOSE!

Would you rather...

be sexually abused by Count Chocula

OR

get bukkake'd by the Smurfs?

Things to consider: Papa, Hefty, Clumsy, Brainy Smurf's a heavy cummer

YOU MUST CHOOSE!

Would you rather...

have your nipples gnawed off by a swarm of fire ants

OR

sit on an umbrella and then open it?

Would you rather...

have your genitals drawn and quartered

OR

have your urinary tract filled with cement?

YOU MUST CHOOSE!

Would you rather...

receive an enema with leech–infested water

OR

dry-hump a cheese grater naked?

Would you rather...

stick your schlong in the spokes of a spinning bike wheel *OR* an electrical outlet?

a George Foreman Grill turned all the way up *OR* a car door right before slamming it?

a tank full of hungry piranhas *OR* a paper shredder?

in a bowl of liquid nitrogen lubricant *OR* on a tee for a Tiger Woods drive?

YOU MUST CHOOSE!

Would you rather...

get your labia stuck to a flagpole in the middle of winter

OR

be manually stimulated by the man with the world's longest fingernails?

YOU MUST CHOOSE!

Would you rather...

all of your drunken phone calls be recorded and played back on a popular radio station

OR

have all your love letters and emails posted on AOL's homepage?

Would you rather...

perform oral sex on a chronic flatulator

OR

give Forest Whitaker a handjob?

YOU MUST CHOOSE!

You are searching through your parent's closet.
Would you rather find...

cocaine *OR* a list of swinger clubs with grades written next to each listing?

Nina Hartley's *Guide to Anal Sex OR* your adoption papers?

edible undies *OR* copies of love letters from your mom to Baron Von Raschke?

YOU MUST CHOOSE!

Would you rather...

be double-teamed by mimes

OR

be wagon-trained by a quartet of sex-starved Ewoks?

Would you rather...

find a used condom at the bottom of your vanilla latte

OR

find a dirty panty liner under the cheese in your tuna melt?

YOU MUST CHOOSE!

Would you rather...

be donkey-punched by King Kong Bundy

OR

be arabian goggled by Mr. Miyagi?

Things to consider: what we have done with our elite college education

YOU MUST CHOOSE!

Would you rather be caught masturbating by...

your grandparents *OR* your parents?

a one year old *OR* your dog?

HR Pufnstuf *OR* the ghost of Harriet Tubman?

YOU MUST CHOOSE!

Would you rather...

as a guy, be licking a woman's breast only to discover a 3 inch hair on her nipple

OR

be kissing her lower back only to discover a tattoo of Roger Ebert?

Would you rather...

make out with someone in a dark club only to find when the lights go on that their mouth is covered in open puss-filled cold sores

OR

that it's your mother-in-law? Father-in-law? Bill Wennington?

YOU MUST CHOOSE!

Would you rather...

have your mom bring a blacklight into your room to reveal the various sexual fluids strewn about

OR

have to call tech support because you were surfing porn and more and more porn sites and pop-ups keep coming up on screen and so you have to talk through the problem with specifics and you're like "this website Assparade.com comes up and when I try to close it, an ad for Peter North's Volume pills comes up," and your mom comes in, and you try to close all the sites and ads real quick, like you're playing missile command on Atari, but every time you close a window, another porn ad pops open, and it's like trying to cut off the Hydra's heads, and you turn off the monitor but it's too late, and you realize that maybe it's time to move out of your parents' house?

YOU MUST CHOOSE!

65

Would you rather...

find out your spouse has herpes

OR

that they are having an affair? With Tito Santana?! "(Play ominous music here)

YOU MUST CHOOSE!

Would you rather...

watch a stripper who visibly suffers from severe arthritis *OR* who is stricken with problem flatulence?

who is 60 pounds overweight *OR* who dances with a Hitler theme?

with protruding varicose veins *OR* who eerily resembles Tommy Lasorda?

YOU MUST CHOOSE!

ng sex, would you rather hear...

h" OR "What is that?!"?

~~ops~~" OR "That's where that is"?

a yawn OR "Oy Vey"?

nervous laughter OR maniacal laughter?

"Must kill president" OR "Circuit malfunction"?

YOU MUST CHOOSE!

Would you rather...

receive oral sex from the subject in Edvard Munch's "The Scream"

OR

commit lewd acts on Teddy Ruxpin?

YOU MUST CHOOSE!

website broadcast all your showers

your bowel movements?

YOU MUST CHOOSE!

Fight for your love...

Sure, you're a lover not a fighter, but the Deity wants to see that you'd fight for your loved one. He's kidnapped your significant other and says you must defeat his minions gladiator-style in a fight to the death in a closed 20' by 20' room. All enemies are hostile.

Would you rather fight to the death...

50 remote control planes *OR* 1000 hamsters?

800 sloths *OR* 80 penguins?

possessed office supplies *OR* possessed deli meats?

Koala bears *OR* Berenstain Bears?

25,000,000 starving ringworms *OR* the starting line-up for the New York Liberty?

YOU MUST CHOOSE!

71

This Or That?

Challenge yourself or your friends with the following quiz.
Answers are on page 168.

1. Supreme Court Justice or Venereal Disease?
   a. Scalia
   b. Gonorrhea
   c. Chlamydia
   d. Bader Ginsburg

2. Bible Chapter or Porn Magazine?
   a. Revelation
   b. Cheri
   c. Genesis
   d. Barely Legal

YOU MUST CHOOSE!

This Or That? (continued)

3. Batman Villain or Dildo?
    a. The Penguin
    b. The Emperor
    c. The Joker
    d. The Tickler
    e. Mr. Softee
    f. Two-face

4. Catskills Comedian or VD Symptom?
    a. Clammy Hands
    b. Shecky Green
    c. Swollen Glands
    d. Soupy Sales

5. 80's Movie or Euphemism for Sex?
    a. Romancing the Stone
    b. Bumping Uglies
    c. Gleaming the Cube
    d. Burying the Purple Headed Warrior

YOU MUST CHOOSE!

WOULD YOU...

The Deity, in addition to being vengeful and sadistic, is lazy. So lazy in fact that he didn't even bother to finish his catchphrase. The result is the more abbreviated but just as thought-provoking "Would You..?"

Would you... have sex with a 70 year old Marlon Brando to have sex with a 30 year old Marlon Brando?

Would you... have sex with a walrus to have sex with all the Playmates of the current year (men); with *People*'s 50 Sexiest Men (women)?

Would you... have sex with John Daly daily, to have sex with Keira Knightly, nightly?

YOU MUST CHOOSE!

Would you... make out with and feverishly grope your best friend's mom for forty minutes for $15,000?

Would you... want a second portable set of "voo-doo doll" genitalia that communicates all sensation to your real genitalia?
Things to consider: theft, pets, surreptitious self-pleasure

Would you... have sex with someone who had a perfect body of the opposite sex but has your face?

YOU MUST CHOOSE!

Would you... give a hickey to your grandmother for $5000?

Would you... want to be able to perform oral sex on yourself?

Things to consider: never wanting to leave the house, which leads to lack of exercise, which leads to weight gain, which leads to no longer being able to continue said ability

Would you... submerge your balls in boiling water for 10 seconds to have a 10 second glimpse of creation?

YOU MUST CHOOSE!

Would you... dry-hump Neal Patrick Harris for a complete understanding of badminton strategy?

Would you... spend two weeks wearing nothing but a g-string and Tevas for $2,000?

Would you... give up 2 years of your life to have a penis that was 3 inches longer (men) or breasts that were 3 sizes larger (women)?

YOU MUST CHOOSE!

Would you... take the surname of your spouse upon marriage if it were "Vulvatron?"

Would you... add a "De" to the beginning of your first name (men)/change the last syllable of your first name to "eesha" (women) to be able to orgasm three times as intensely?

Would you... as a man, get D-Cup breast implants for $100,000?
(They can be removed after a year.)

YOU MUST CHOOSE!

Let's get right to the point.

Would you... bang the Michelin Man for a 64 inch flat screen plasma TV?

YOU MUST CHOOSE!

Would you... let a stranger have sex with your spouse for $100,000 dollars? $500,000? $2,000,000? What if that stranger was former NBA great Ralph Sampson?

Would you... bludgeon thirty baby seals to death to have sex with Penelope Cruz? Vice-versa?

Would you... butter Eric Montross to be impervious to tan lines?

YOU MUST CHOOSE!

(for men) **Would you...** dance with a woman if you knew it would never lead to sex?

Would you... dedicate a book to your mothers if the book was full of vile, infantile and prurient material including the phrase "wagon-trained by a quartet of sex-starved Ewoks"?

Would you... fondle Renaldo Nehemiah for a new velvet jumpsuit?

YOU MUST CHOOSE!

chapter SIX

DATING AND MARRIAGE

Dating and marriage, much like the workings of the Deity, often seem to unfold according to reasons beyond our understanding. Consequently, the Deity feels you could use a little direction when it comes to such matters. Of course, always a believer in free will, he allows you the ultimate choice.

Would you rather...

marry the spouse of your dreams but gain 10 pounds a year
OR
have them gain 10 pounds a year?

Would you rather...

have a lover who is 6'3 tall with a 3 inch penis *OR* 5'2 tall with a 9 inch penis?

7' tall with a 1 inch penis *OR* 2' tall with a 12 inch penis?

18' tall with a 4 inch penis *OR* 1' tall with a 64 inch penis?

YOU MUST CHOOSE!

Would you rather...

date someone with a razor sharp wit

OR

a vibrating tongue?

Would you rather...

only be able to pick up guys/chicks via middle school style notes folded
with hearts

OR

by window-side serenades of hits from the early '80s?

Things to consider: *Total Eclipse of the Heart, All Out of Love, Turning Japanese, Rocket*

YOU MUST CHOOSE!

87

Would you rather...

date someone with a winterbush (very heavy unkempt pubic hair)

OR

an autumnbush (hair that changes color in the fall)?

Would you rather...

marry someone whose desired personal space was 2 inches

OR

30 feet?

YOU MUST CHOOSE!

Would you rather...

your Lamaze coach be that excitable Spanish soccer announcer

OR

Jesse Jackson?

Would you rather...

your marriage counselor be Dr. Drew

OR

Dr. Dre?

YOU MUST CHOOSE!

89

Would you rather...

have your wedding planned by Kim Jong-Il

OR

Jokey Smurf?

Things to consider: gifts

WOULD YOU RATHER...? LOVE & SEX

Would you rather...

have your wedding planned by Kim Jong-Il

OR

Jokey Smurf?

Things to consider: gifts

YOU MUST CHOOSE!

Would you rather have your love life written by...

Ally McBeal creator David E. Kelly **OR** porn czar Seymoore Butts?

Woody Allen **OR** Nicholas Sparks?

Charles Bukowski **OR** Sir Mix-A-Lot?
Things to consider: honesty pertaining to advocating of large posterior, tendency of other brothers to fabricate

YOU MUST CHOOSE!

Would you rather marry...

an ugly rock star *OR* a hot garbage man?

a rich, shallow investment banker *OR* a poor, brilliant artist?

a self-righteous milkman *OR* a melancholy locksmith?

a bipolar tour guide *OR* an autistic Foot Locker salesperson?

YOU MUST CHOOSE!

Would you rather...

have your wedding ceremony conducted in the tone of a rap video

OR

in the tone of an elementary school play?

YOU MUST CHOOSE!

Would you rather...

date someone who only wants to have sex once a month

OR

date someone who made you solve a riddle before moving to each new step sexually?

Things to consider: what is the angle between the hands of a clock if the clock shows 3:15? If you answered, "7.5 degrees," you may now fondle my breasts.

YOU MUST CHOOSE!

Indecent Proposals

Would you rather be proposed to...

in the New York Times crossword puzzle *OR* with skywriting?

at Circuit City *OR* at Del Taco?

in a robot imitation *OR* written backwards in blood on the wall?

on the jumbotron screen at a baseball game *OR* be divorced on the jumbotron screen at a baseball game?

YOU MUST CHOOSE!

Would you rather...

spend your honeymoon in a Home Depot *OR* a bowling alley?

in a slaughterhouse *OR* at your mom's house?

at a four day Civil War re-enactment *OR* at a Vietnam War re-enactment ?

YOU MUST CHOOSE!

For your wedding, would you rather...

be registered at Quiznos *OR* at the Chuck E Cheese prize counter?

an S&M shop *OR* a D&D shop?

Leo's House of Gauze *OR* All Things Tungsten?

YOU MUST CHOOSE!

Would you rather date...

a woman who loves to give oral sex, but while doing it, hums the tune to the *Sanford and Son* theme song

OR

a woman who talks filthy but speaks in the voice of Yosemite Sam?

Would you rather date...

a woman with a great body but simple conversations skills

OR

a woman who speaks with wit and insight but keeps her hand perpetually soaking in a bowl of wet spinach?

YOU MUST CHOOSE!

Would you rather...

draw your dating pool from people browsing the Self Help section of the book store

OR

the Sci-Fi section?

YOU MUST CHOOSE!

Would you rather...

when you get a prospective date's number or e-mail, only be able to write it down by tattooing it on your body

OR

your only pick-up line be: "To answer your question—Yes. Light weights, high reps."?

YOU MUST CHOOSE!

The Deity has released a line of new colognes.

Would you rather wear...

New Tennis Ball *OR* Wet German Shepherd?

Mulch *OR* Pungent Reefer?

Eau de Gomberg *OR* Eau de Heimberg?

YOU MUST CHOOSE!

Would you rather date...

a prop comedian *OR* a compulsive air guitarist?

a half-woman/half horse *OR* a half-woman/half-couch?

someone with a farmer's tan *OR* an inverse farmer's tan?

YOU MUST CHOOSE!

On a first date with someone you really like, would you rather...

be unable to talk about anything other than the mechanism that causes grass stains

OR

have to use the phrase "white power" 20 times?

YOU MUST CHOOSE!

Would you rather...

have your wedding vows written by gangsta rappers

OR

by the author of one of those African spam money request emails?

Things to consider: "It is of the utmost Urgency with which I submit this plea for your sincerest Love and Trustworthiness?"

YOU MUST CHOOSE!

For your wedding, would you rather...

have a paintball war at the reception

OR

enter down the aisle to the tune of "We're Not Gonna Take It" by Twisted Sister?

YOU MUST CHOOSE!

chapter SEVEN

GETTING PERSONAL

It's your turn to play Deity. Challenge your friends with these personalizable dilemmas.

Would you rather...

play strip poker with (insert three relatives)

OR

rub oil on every inch of (insert vile acquaintance)?

Would you rather...

call up (insert set of friend's parents), state your name, and have phone sex

OR

take a shower with (insert somebody else's parents)?

YOU MUST CHOOSE!

Would you rather...

be caught masturbating by (insert friend of the family)

OR

catch (insert friend of the family) masturbating?

Would you rather...

have reciprocal oral sex with (insert unappealing acquaintance)

OR

lose your (insert body part)?

YOU MUST CHOOSE!

Would you rather...

watch (insert two unattractive acquaintances) have sex

OR

get a 7 minute lap dance by (insert friend's parent)?

YOU MUST CHOOSE!

Would you rather...

have (insert friend or relative) pose naked until you have painted a reasonably accurate portrait

OR

meticulously moisturize, massage, and talc (insert unattractive person)?

YOU MUST CHOOSE!

Would you rather...

engage in heavy petting with (insert head of state)

OR

dry hump (insert political satirist)?

Would you rather...

play (insert board game) with (insert hot celebrity)

OR

(insert verb) with a (insert adjective) (insert former NFL wide receiver)?

YOU MUST CHOOSE!

"Would you rather's" you can test!

Much of what we write is very "Do not try this at home." But here are some perfectly healthy ideas when tried in the safety and privacy of your own home.

When receiving cunnilingus, would you rather have the man use his tongue to spell out...

the cursive English alphabet *OR* non-cursive capital letters?

the phrase "I am the greatest" *OR* "Milton is incorrigible"?

the Hebrew alphabet *OR* tap out Morse Code?

YOU MUST CHOOSE!

Here's another fun one to try at home.

Would you rather...

stuff every orifice with dozens of shoe horns and Mr. T dolls while screaming "Resistance is Futile"

OR

dress up like a conquistador while bakers whip you with baguettes and pour battery acid on your nipples, all while you malign the current French administration?

YOU MUST CHOOSE!

Survey Says

The following are results from polls taken on our website
www.wouldyourather.com <http://www.wouldyourather.com/>.
The questions are from *Would You Rather...? 2: Electric Boogaloo*,
available on the website and at stores.

Would you rather...
be compelled to enter every room by jumping into the doorway with an imaginary
pistol drawn, like the star of a 70's cop show – 62%

OR

invariably make your orgasm face instead of smiling when being photographed? – 38%

Would you rather...
be a crash test dummy – 41%

OR

a fluffer for animal nature documentaries? – 59%

YOU MUST CHOOSE!

Would you rather...

be able to consume fatty foods without gaining weight - 77%

OR

be able to have unprotected sex without getting sexual diseases? - 23%

Things to consider: herpes, gravy fries, cheese balls

Would you rather...

never be able to experience orgasm - 48%

OR

perpetually experience orgasm? - 52%

YOU MUST CHOOSE!

Mixed Blessings

Would you rather...

be incredibly charming, but only when discussing your bowel movements

OR

have an infallible pick-up line, but only with Fuddruckers employees?

Would you rather...

be found attractive by all members of the opposite sex, but secrete copious amounts of steak sauce when aroused

OR

have chocolate flavored genitals, but have all your offspring be exact clones of Walter Matthau?

YOU MUST CHOOSE!

Would you rather...

have charming dimples but have to forever and exclusively use the email address scrotiescrote@hotmail.com

OR

have a twinkle in your eye, but be engaged to someone that swears s/he is the reincarnation of Oliver Cromwell (and passes a lie detector test to prove it)?

YOU MUST CHOOSE!

Would you rather have sex with...

this guy

OR

this guy?

YOU MUST CHOOSE!

chapter EIGHT

THE DEITY'S GREATEST HITS: VOLUME 3: ELECTRIC BOOGALOO 2

The Deity was cleaning out the recesses of his depraved imagination and found a few more quandaries amidst the mess. The result: 45 pages of variable quality dilemmas.

Would you rather...

have a scrotum that fills with fresh-popped popcorn upon getting aroused (à la Jiffy Pop)

OR

make the sound of a foghorn upon orgasm?

Would you rather...

be incapable of moving your body once sexually turned on

OR

be completely infertile except when inside churches?

YOU MUST CHOOSE!

Would you rather have sex with...

Chelsea Clinton *OR* a jaundiced Sandra Bullock?

an albino Freddie Prinze, Jr. *OR* a severely sun-burnt Matt LeBlanc?

a 400 pound person on top *OR* a 300 pound person on crack?

a Chinese version of Courtney Cox *OR* a black version of Reese Witherspoon?

WWE's Chyna *OR* Mandy Moore if she was missing an arm? Both arms? And a leg? Just a torso and a head?

Would you rather...

have breasts that age ten times faster than the rest of your body

OR

have no feeling whatsoever in your genital regions, except when touched by people over the age of 70?

YOU MUST CHOOSE!

Would you rather...

have pornographic pop-up ads constantly appearing in your thoughts

OR

have your cell phone wired into your body with the ring function set on "orgasm"?

Things to consider: driving, getting work done; actually, the first option is pretty much how it is with men

Would you rather...

watch *Girls Gone Wild*

OR

Rabbis Gone Wild?

YOU MUST CHOOSE!

Would you rather...

lactate spider webbing *OR* Milwaukee's Best?

holy water *OR* penicillin?

air pressure *OR* spray paint?
Things to consider: pumping tires, balls, foreplay

Would you rather live in a world...

where corporate hold music was replaced with phone sex
OR
where Casual Friday was preceded by Thong Thursday?

YOU MUST CHOOSE!

Would you rather have a threesome with...

Karl Rove and Sally Struthers *OR* Carrot Top and Margaret Thatcher?

Kate Hudson and Rey Mysterio, Jr *OR* Ed Bradley and Amber Lynn?

Wolf Blitzer and Liv Tyler *OR* your significant other and Arnold Palmer's caddie?

Would you rather...

have your entire sexual history be re-enacted by the animatronic robots in a Disney World ride á la the Pirates of the Caribbean?

OR

have the moments and characters in your sex life released by the Franklin Mint as a commemorative chess set?

YOU MUST CHOOSE!

Would you rather have...

9 inch nipples *OR* a 9 inch clitoris?

a 24 month menstrual cycle *OR* a 24 hour menstrual cycle?

a 4 pound tongue *OR* a 4 pound testicle?

Would you rather have sex with...

Maroon 5 *OR* Blink 182?

Sum 51 *OR* Matchbox 20?

Front 242 *OR* Florp 968?

YOU MUST CHOOSE!

Would you rather...

have your mom have to put on your condoms like she was dressing you as a child for the winter

OR

never be able to call your spouse by the same name twice (or you will be struck dead by the Lord)?

Things to consider: coming up with new terms of endearment – Honey, Baby, Schnookeylups, Porko, Flartran, Sweetballs, Fatooshk

Would you rather your pimp be...

Strom Thurmond *OR* Emmanuel Lewis?

Grimace *OR* Chewbacca?

Vijay Singh *OR* Beetle Bailey?

YOU MUST CHOOSE!

Pick Your Scrotum!

Would you rather have...

a scrotum slightly too small for your testicles or a scrotum that was 40 times bigger than it is currently? (testicles remain the same size)

a transparent scrotum or a denim scrotum?

a plaid scrotum or a bungie-scrotum™

Things to consider: other books that have an entire page dedicated to the scrotum: James Joyce's *Ulysses*, *Goodnight Moon*, the *Bible*, Jane Austen's *Scrotum*

YOU MUST CHOOSE!

Would you... perform oral sex on (insert undesirable acquaintance) to have sex with (insert celebrity)?

Would you rather...

tag on the phrase "for a girl" to every compliment you give a female
OR
tag on a sarcastic "Sherlock" to every sexual exclamation you utter?

YOU MUST CHOOSE!

Would you rather...

be able to make your pubic hair grow in the pasta variety of your choice

OR

have the power to induce carnal fantasies about
Nicolas Corpernicus?

Things to consider: rotini, penne, manicotti, macchio

YOU MUST CHOOSE!

Would you rather...

turn into Rip Taylor when masturbating

OR

have your sexual appetite vary directly with proximity to Radio Shack?

Would you rather...

have to use condoms that come in a wrapper where you have to finish the crossword puzzle before it can be opened

OR

be unable to shake the image of Meadowlark Lemon during all sexual congress?

YOU MUST CHOOSE!

Would you rather have breast implants made of...

attracting magnets *OR* repelling magnets?

locusts *OR* throbbing hearts?

coffee grinds *OR* the spirit of Malcolm X?

YOU MUST CHOOSE!

Would you rather...

have troll doll heads for nipples

OR

pipe cleaners for pubic hair?

Would you rather...

see an opera based on your love life

OR

a porno based on your sex life?

YOU MUST CHOOSE!

Would you rather have sex with...

The Tin Man *OR* The Scarecrow?

Mr. Belvedere *OR* Matlock?

your dentist *OR* your 3rd grade PE teacher?

the "Where's the Beef" lady *OR* the "I've fallen and I can't get up!" lady?

Skeletor *OR* Gargamel?

YOU MUST CHOOSE!

Would you rather...

be bisexually attracted to men and fish

OR

tri-sexually attracted to men, women, and boxes of Milk Duds?

YOU MUST CHOOSE!

Would you rather...

be required to file an official request with the federal government in order to receive oral sex

OR

have "Total number of sexual partners" be a required box to fill out on every job application?

YOU MUST CHOOSE!

Would you rather...

utter all sexual explanations with a British *OR* Mexican accent?

in an interrogative inflection *OR* through a ventriloquist dummy?

in beat-box *OR* Haiku?

Things to Consider:
oh yeah do me yeah
like willow reed in cool pond
pinch my nipple

YOU MUST CHOOSE!

Breastify!

Would you rather...

have 1 breast *OR* 3 breasts?

inverted concave breasts *OR* roving breasts?

snow globes for breasts *OR* magic 8-Balls?

the living heads of Cheech and Chong *OR* crystal balls where you can see the future (but only of the carpet industry)?

YOU MUST CHOOSE!

Would you rather...

have testicles with the density of hydrogen

OR

prematurely ejaculate by two weeks?

YOU MUST CHOOSE!

Would you rather be unable to distinguish between...

hands and ears *OR* nipples and the TV remote control?

the phrases "I love you" and "goodbye" *OR* your significant other and Jim Lehrer?

your bedroom and Jamba Juice *OR* the texture "smooth" and the concept of "ambivalence"?

YOU MUST CHOOSE!

When you sleep, would you rather...

instead of REM (rapid eye movement), experience WTL (wild tongue lapping) *OR* have your penis move like a windshield wiper?

be a sleepwalker *OR* a sleephumper?

experience nocturnal tumescence *OR* nocturnal luminescence?

YOU MUST CHOOSE!

Would you rather...

receive a Cleveland Steamer from Tom Snyder

OR

a Dirty Sanchez from former Postmaster General Marvin Runyon?

Would you rather...

have a horizontal buttcrack

OR

vertically aligned breasts?

YOU MUST CHOOSE!

(Dr. Seuss fans only)

Would you rather have sex with...

Salma Hayek on a kayak

OR

Halle Berry on a ferry? Penelope Cruz in grey ooze?

YOU MUST CHOOSE!

You live with a roommate. You decide to use a blacklight to check your room for hidden "stains."

Would you rather find stains all over...

your washcloth *OR* your favorite cereal bowl?

your computer keyboard and mouse *OR* a framed photo of your family?

your copy of *Would You Rather...? Love&Sex* *OR* your copy of George Washington Carver's biography?

YOU MUST CHOOSE!

The Deity is going to give you an outfit to spice things up in the bedroom.

Would you rather...

wear bologna lingerie

OR

aviator glasses, crotchless acid wash jeans, and a giant foam rubber "you're number one" hand?

YOU MUST CHOOSE!

Pick Your Vagina!

Would you rather have a vagina...

that acts as a guillotine 1 out of every 8 times an object is inserted *OR* one that secretes sulfuric acid upon orgasm?

that doubles as a trash compactor *OR* a cassette player?

that howls like a wolf when the moon is full *OR* one that randomly belts out Sinatra tunes?

YOU MUST CHOOSE!

Would you rather...

have the sexual skills, know-how, and dexterity of a 13 year old

OR

a 70 year old?

Would you rather...

awaken from a drunken one-night stand only to realize you slept with your best friend's mother

OR

come down from drug-induced hallucinations only to realize you slept with Haystacks Calhoun?

Things to consider: projected audience for this question: 4

YOU MUST CHOOSE!

Would you rather...

ejaculate hot coffee

OR

crazy glue?

YOU MUST CHOOSE!

Would you rather...

have sex with Diana Ross *OR* a 200% scale Denise Richards?

Maria Bartiromo *OR* a blurry Catherine Zeta Jones?

a drunk Tara Reid *OR* a Jennifer Love Hewitt who won't shut up about her trip to Colonial Williamsburg?

Will Smith after undergoing a sex change *OR* Sarah Michelle Gellar 10 seconds after she gives birth?

everyone you know with a surname starting with "B" *OR* "W"?

Josh Hartnett *OR* Gary Coleman if they exchanged heights?

Hugh Grant *OR* Mr. T if they switched voices and demeanors?

YOU MUST CHOOSE!

Would you rather have...

15 fingers *OR* 3 tongues?

57 testicles *OR* 1 testicle the size of a honeydew?

no nipples *OR* 11 nipples?

Things to consider: Reread now as "Would you rather date someone who had..."

YOU MUST CHOOSE!

Would you rather have sex with...

just the top half of Briana Banks *OR* just the bottom half of Britney Spears?

a Filipino Justin Timberlake *OR* a Caucasian Samuel L Jackson?

Clint Howard *OR* Kate Beckinsale, 10 seconds after she passed away?

Topher Grace *OR* Kevin James?
If they exchanged weights?

Valerie Bertinelli with a glass eye *OR* Agatha Christie
with 42DD breasts?

YOU MUST CHOOSE!

The Deity encourages adventure in the bedroom between two consenting adults. You and your significant other are to participate in a role-playing fantasy...

Would you rather fantasize the scenario of...

"Rugged Cowboy Discovers Handmaiden in the Barn" *OR* "Cheerleader Approaches Bookish Professor After Class"?

"Secretary and Boss Working Late" *OR* "Tax Session with Accountant Ignites Passions"?

"Fan Meets Post-Concert Fabio" *OR* "Cashier Bumps Into Anonymous Thin Moroccan In Arby's Bathroom Stall"?

YOU MUST CHOOSE!

Would you rather...

spend two romantically charged hours with Maria Navratolova

OR

get a lap dance by a sleestack from *Land of the Lost*?

YOU MUST CHOOSE!

Would you rather...

have phone sex with the teacher from the old Charlie Brown specials

OR

have telegraph sex? (see below for example)

PHONE SEX OPERATOR : I'm so horny STOP

YOU: What are you wearing STOP

PHONE SEX OPERATOR: Nothing STOP I'm so horny STOP

YOU: Oh yeah? STOP... (silence) No, I mean, don't stop. STOP... (silence)...
Shit...

YOU MUST CHOOSE!

Pick Your Pubes!

You can pick your friends, and you can pick your pubes, but you can't... wait, how does that go? Anyway...

Would you rather...

wear your pubic hair in a Fu-Manchu style *OR* ZZ Top beard style?

have pubes that lit up like fiber optic wires *OR* pubic hair comprised of Brillo?

have pubic hair that changes color to match your shirt *OR* pubes that grow "up" and around your body like ivy on a house?

YOU MUST CHOOSE!

Would you rather...

attract swarms of fireflies when aroused

OR

have the sound of microphone feedback intermittently emanating from your crotch?

Would you rather...

have gratuitous Ted Danson cameos during erotic dreams

OR

be able to only have sex on bumper pool tables?

YOU MUST CHOOSE!

Would you rather...

have sex with a a woman with Kathy Bates's body on the top half and Carmen Electra's body on the bottom half

OR

Carmen Electra's on top and Kathy Bates's body on the bottom?

YOU MUST CHOOSE!

Would you rather always have to wear...

a spiked collar and black leather cap *OR* cherry Twizzler nipple piercings?

no underwear *OR* Green Lantern Underoos?

a sombrero *OR* a 5 pound Prince Albert?

Would you rather...

have an 8 inch wide innie belly-button

OR

have a 10 inch long outie belly button?

YOU MUST CHOOSE!

Actor or Character?

Would you rather...

have sex with Harrison Ford OR Han Solo?

Sean Penn OR Jeff Spicoli?

Hugh Jackman OR Wolverine?

Jeff Bridges OR Starman and The Dude (Jeff Lebowski) together?

Angelina Jolie OR Lara Croft?

Douglas Rain OR Hal9000?

YOU MUST CHOOSE!

Would you rather...

only be sexually aroused by people experiencing engine trouble

OR

having severe allergic reactions?

Things to consider: cruising highways, cruising hospitals

Would you rather live in a world where...

penis size fluctuates with interest rates

OR

where romantic moments were magically scored by a Journey soundtrack?

YOU MUST CHOOSE!

Upon climax, would you rather...

shout out the names of various US Presidents *OR* Zagat's restaurant reviews?

the chorus to "Hava Nagila" *OR* the chorus to "Whoomp! There It Is"?

Monster Manual descriptions *OR* those from *Deities & Demigods*?

Would You Rather...? questions *OR* Barry Larkin's career statistics?

YOU MUST CHOOSE!

Would you rather have sex with...

Batman *OR* Super Man?

The Flash *OR* Spiderman?

Toucan Sam *OR* Cap'n Crunch?
Things to consider: Cap'n Crunch's penchant for buggery

Would you rather have sex with...

The Bionic Woman *OR* Wilma from *Buck Rogers*?

Wonder Woman *OR* a real-life anatomically correct Barbie?

Snow White *OR* Rapunzel?
Things to consider: likely Rapunzel winterbush

YOU MUST CHOOSE!

Would you rather...

play this book with Adam Corrola

OR

John Ashcroft?

Would you rather have your only means of foreplay be...

cheek-kissing *OR* joint-fondling?

firm handshakes *OR* the ferocious tonguing of eyeballs?

political debate *OR* *Three's Company*–like misunderstandings?

YOU MUST CHOOSE!

Would you rather...

your penis (men)/breasts (women) increase in size by ten percent each year

OR

decrease in size by two percent each year?

Would you rather...

speak in the voice of a possessed Linda Blair in *The Exorcist* during sex

OR

compulsively yell out Starbucks orders in the heat of passion?
(for example, "Oh, yeah, oh yeah... Double Decaf Iced Mocha Frap!")

YOU MUST CHOOSE!

Would you rather...

always orgasm thirty seconds into sex

OR

only be able to orgasm after three hours of continuous sex?

Would you rather...

vicariously experience all orgasms that occur in your zip code

OR

during sex, have the Microsoft paper clip help icon appear with sex tips?

YOU MUST CHOOSE!

Answer Key
Answers to *Pornification*

1. American Beauty
2. City Slickers
3. Finding Nemo
4. The Slutty Professor
5. T.W.A.T
6. Sex Toy Story or Boy Story
7. Big Trouble in Little Vagina
8. Analize This
9. Glory Hole
10. Face Jam
11. Malcolm XXX
12. Titty Titty Gang Bang
13. Shaft
14. Cold Mountin'
15. Lou Dobbs Money Shot

Answers to **This or That?**

1. **a.** Supreme Court Justice **b.** Venereal Disease
   c. Venereal Disease **d.** Supreme Court Justice

2. **a.** Bible Chapter **b.** Porn Magazine
   c. Both **d.** Porn Magazine

3. **a.** Batman Villain **b.** Dildo
   c. Batman Villain **d.** Dildo
   e. Dildo **f.** Batman Villain

4. **a.** VD Symptom **b.** Catskills Comedian
   c. VD Symptom **d.** Catskills Comedian

5. **a.** '80's Movie **b.** Euphemism for Sex
   c. '80's Movie **d.** Euphemism for Sex

Answers to **Mystery Quiz**

1. Malted milk balls
2. 200 mg
3. False
4. Ed Begley, Jr.
5. Ed Begley, Sr.
6. No, thank you.
7. See 1, 4.

Coming Soon!
Other *Would You Rather...?* books by the authors

Wouldn't You Rather..: Over 200 Pointed Questions to Answer

Sample question: **Wouldn't you rather...** go to the beach than the mountains?

Things to consider: I mean, really, it's obvious, isn't it? Sun? Surf? Jeez!

Would You Rather...? Australia

Sample question: **Would you rather...** take a walkabout with bunyips and yowies in nothing but your stubbies *OR* get in a barney with a fair-dinkum yobbo?

Things to consider: chooks, dunny-buggies

Would You Rather...? Mormon Edition

Sample question: **Would you rather...** marry a Mormon spouse, thereby sealing your eternal place in the Celestial Kingdom *OR* be allowed to drink coffee?

About the Authors

Justin Heimberg is an author and screenwriter living in suburban Maryland.

David Gomberg, had he been on earth, would have been a doctor, a mechanic, a scientist and a warrior. But on Cybertron, there is no difference between these professions. So Gomberg uses his skills to heal and repair—which are the same things to Autobots—to improve the world around him and, if necessary, to fight. Both in power and intelligence, he has no equal. He has the personality of an Abraham Lincoln. He can be immensely kind and his compassion extends to all that lives, including the creatures of Earth. Yet he will battle unceasingly to protect the weak and defend what he believes in. To accomplish this, Gomberg knows that the Decepticons must be defeated for all time.

About the Deity

The ringmaster/MC/overlord of the *Would You Rather...* empire is "the Deity." Psychologically and physically a cross between Charles Manson and Gabe Kaplan, the Deity is the one responsible for creating and presenting the WYR dilemmas. It is the Deity who asks "**Would you rather... watch a porno movie with your parents or a porno movie starring your parents?**" And it is the Deity who orders, without exception, that you must choose. No one knows exactly why he does this; suffice to say, it's for reasons beyond your understanding. The Deity communicates with you not through speech, nor telepathy, but rather through several sharp blows to the stomach that vary in power and location. Nearly omnipotent, often ruthless, and obsessed with former NBA seven-footers, the Deity is a random idea generator with a peculiar predilection for intervening in your life in the strangest ways.

Check out
www.wouldyourather.com

- More Books

- Calendars

- The Board Game

- Bulk quantity discounts

- Comedy

- Contests

- And/or More!